The Magic School Bus®

GETS ALL DRIED UP

A BOOK ABOUT DESERTS

SCHOLASTIC INC.

New York   Toronto   London   Auckland   Sydney
Mexico City   New Delhi   Hong Kong   Buenos Aires

From an episode of the animated TV series
produced by Scholastic Entertainment Inc.
Based on *The Magic School Bus* books
written by Joanna Cole and illustrated by Bruce Degen.

TV tie-in book adaptation by Suzanne Weyn and illustrated by Nancy Stevenson.
TV script written by Brian Meehl and Jocelyn Stevenson.

ISBN 0-590-50831-8

24 23 22 21 20 19 18 17 16 15 14 13   4 5 6 7 8 9/0

Printed in the U.S.A.

Ms. Frizzle is the strangest, most surprising teacher ever. But this morning everything was amazingly calm. We were working on our diorama of the desert. Things seemed normal — which was odd. Nothing is *ever* normal for long in Ms. Frizzle's class!

Most of us thought the diorama looked great, but Tim wasn't happy with it. "There's something missing," he said.

We had sand, gravel, and cacti. We even had a heat lamp for desert sun and a fan for wind. What could possibly have been missing?

"I know!" Phoebe cried. "We need desert animals!"

Ms. Frizzle looked up from what she was doing. "Dynamic deduction, Phoebe!" she said with a smile.

Luckily for us, Ms. Frizzle had exactly what we needed —
a giant barrel full of toy desert animals!

Phoebe lugged the barrel over to the diorama. While she put
the animals into place, Dorothy Ann told us what they were.

"Tortoise, coyote, kangaroo rat, roadrunner, Gila monster . . ."
There were desert animals of all shapes and sizes!

The animals looked really cool. But Carlos didn't think they'd be able to survive in the hot, dry desert.

"There's almost no water in the desert! No water! No food! No shelter!" he said.

Phoebe gasped.

"Scarcity is the name of the game, Pheebs. In no time at all, our cute little animals will be buzzard bait," explained Carlos.

"The poor things!" cried Phoebe. She climbed onto a chair. "We've got to take a stand! Form a committee! We'll call ourselves . . . S.A.D.S."

"S.A.D.S. stands for Students *Against* *Desert* *Scarcity*," Phoebe declared. "Scarcity because food and water is hard to find in the desert."

"Maybe we should take a field trip," Arnold suggested.

Everybody looked at Arnold. Usually, he *hates* field trips. But this time, he was prepared. He carried a bag full of equipment. He was dressed from head to toe in desert gear. And he was reading a field trip survival guide!

Ms. Frizzle got that funny gleam in her eyes. She is *always* ready for a field trip.

Before we knew it, we were aboard the Magic School Bus, heading for the desert.

What do you have in the knapsack, anyway?

Oh, a little sunblock, a snake bite kit, a few dozen Malloblasters . . .

Suddenly, the school bus started zooming down the road. Faster . . . faster . . . then, all at once, the bus changed into a plane! We lifted off the ground and soared over some mountains.

Phoebe looked worried. "Ms. Frizzle," she said, "this isn't a desert! These are mountains! We must be going the wrong way."

The Friz shook her head. "If it weren't for these mountains, Phoebe, there wouldn't even be a desert."

"Haven't you guys ever heard of the rain shadow effect," Carlos asked.

Nobody had — except Ms. Frizzle, of course. So Carlos explained it to us.

"When warm moist air rises over the mountains," he said, "its water vapor condenses into rain or snow. So it rains and snows over the mountains, leaving the land on the other side as dry as a desert."

Without warning, Ms. Frizzle leaned on a lever. The bus took a nosedive!

"Aaahhh!" everyone cried. Everyone except Arnold, that is. He was busy reading his field trip survival guide.

"Field Trip Tip Number 63," he read. "In the event of a rapid loss of altitude, you may put on a parachute."

We were about to crash! But the Friz flipped a switch and the school bus changed into an all-terrain desert vehicle. At the very last minute, we rolled to a smooth stop. Whew!

The sun in the desert was hot, hot, hot! We all started to sweat. Except for Ms. Frizzle. She *always* keeps her cool.

Above us, a vulture flew in circles. But Ms. Frizzle didn't seem to notice.

"Come along, class," she said. "We're here to experience the desert! Take chances! Make mistakes! Get dusty!"

Is it just me, or does this look like our *final* field trip?

Come on, guys! We've go to save the animals!

Before long, we spied a hungry roadrunner chasing a collared lizard across the desert sand.

"Quick!" Phoebe exclaimed. "Everyone back on the bus! We have to save that lizard!"

Ms. Frizzle's eyes lit with an idea. "A situation worth exploration, Phoebe!" she said.

Inside the bus, Ms. Frizzle pulled a lever. The bus started shrinking. It turned into a Gila monster! And now the roadrunner was after us!

Ms. Frizzle stepped on the gas pedal . . . hard! "As I always say, when the going gets hungry, the hungry get going."

A few seconds later, the roadrunner scooped us up in his beak! How could we possibly get out of this one? Arnold checked his field trip manual.

"Field Trip Tip Number 107: To avoid being eaten, become inedible," he read. "What does that mean?"

"It means we should become something that can't be eaten," Dorothy Ann explained.

"Do I hear a suggestion to avoid digestion?" asked the Friz. She pulled another lever.

The bus shook like crazy, then turned into a spiky horned lizard! The roadrunner spit us out — fast. It obviously didn't like lizards with spikes.

"So, the little animals here have special ways to avoid being eaten," Phoebe realized, "like being prickly."

"Ah! Phoebe! That's right!" said the Friz.

Next, Phoebe made us all get out to look at a jackrabbit. "Arnold, give it your hat," she said. "How else is he going to keep cool?"

The Friz grinned. "EAR-conditioning." She explained that when the rabbit's warm blood flows through its big ears, the blood cools. Then, the cooled blood flows into the rest of its body.

Next, Phoebe wanted to help a desert tortoise. "How would you like to be a tortoise roasting in the hot desert sun?" she asked.

Ms. Frizzle's eyes glimmered. "As I always say, there's more than one way to beat the heat," she said. "Everyone back into the all-terrain vehicle."

Now, even Arnold looked worried. What would the Friz do next?

Whhirrr! Spin! Shrink, shrink, shrink. The all-terrain vehicle grew a tough shell. Then, it burrowed down, down, down, way under the ground.

"Ah, so this is what it's like to be a desert tortoise," said Ms. Frizzle. She sounded delighted.

A second later, everything went dark.

"Where are we?" Tim shouted.

"In a tortoise burrow. An underground shelter," the Friz explained.

We kept cool in our turtle burrow until the sun went down. When we went back outside — wow! The desert was suddenly a very busy place. It was *full* of animals.

"What happened?" cried Keesha.

Arnold looked at his guide book. "Field Trip Tip Number 57," he read. "To beat the heat, do like most desert animals. Come out only at night."

You don't have any sweaters in that knapsack, do you, Arnold?

Once the sun goes down, the air cools off.

Carlos grinned. "Another way desert animals can help themselves, Phoebe. Let's face it," he said. "S.A.D.S. is a bust."

"All right!" said Phoebe. "Maybe these animals can protect themselves. And maybe they know how to keep cool. But there's one thing I *know* they need . . . water!"

She ran into the bus, grabbed all our water containers, and trudged back out the door.

Oh, no! Phoebe was going to give our precious water to the animals!

"Wait, Phoebe!" Carlos cried. "Maybe they don't need *our* water. They must get water somehow, because they couldn't live without it."

Phoebe frowned. "Okay. If you're so smart, tell me how," she challenged.

As if on cue, something wet splashed Carlos and Phoebe. Rain!

A second later, it was pouring. We all made a dash for the bus.

Rain in the desert?

It doesn't happen very often.

Floooood!

The next morning, the desert was amazing! The whole place was in bloom, and animals were *everywhere*!

"Is this a dream?" Phoebe asked.

"No," said the Friz. "It's the desert after a rainstorm."

It's as if they were waiti[ng] for enough water to bloo[m]

Flower power!

Arnold bent over a big puddle. "There are shrimp in here," he exclaimed.

"Shrimp?" said Phoebe. "In the desert?"

"And pigs, too!" Dorothy Ann added. She pointed to a pig eating a cactus.

"Actually, that's a peccary, a desert relative of pigs," explained the Friz.

"Look!" cried Keesha. "There is water in this cactus!"

Dorothy Ann took a closer look. "According to my observations, this piece of cactus is juicy on the inside and waxy on the outside," she said.

"Hey, maybe that waxy stuff keeps the water in," said Tim thoughtfully.

As I always say, when it pours, the desert stores.

"You were right, Carlos," Phoebe said. "The desert animals don't need us to help them. They're already equipped to live here."

"That's right, Phoebe," said Ms. Frizzle. "Everything that lives here has *adaptations* to help cope with life in the desert."

"You mean plants not needing very much water and soaking it up as quickly as possible are adaptations?" asked Dorothy Ann.

Field Trip Tip Number 999
For those without special desert adaptations, alway travel with a teacher with frizzy red hair . . . hmmr

"Absolutely correct," said the Friz.

"And a lizard having spikes is an adaptation that helps keep you off the menu," said Ralphie.

"And, a turtle burrowing under sand and a jackrabbit having big ears are adaptations for beating the heat," Wanda said.

"Yes," agreed Ms. Frizzle. "All the things that live here have special features — adaptations — for survival." She sighed happily. "It makes so much sense."

By the time we got back to school, we were all *very* tired. Especially Arnold.

"Well, I have to say, except for the part where we almost got eaten," he mumbled wearily, "and the part where we almost burned up in the sun, and the part where we almost drowned in a flood . . . my field trip manual was REALLY helpful."

"Well, now that I know all these plants and animals have adaptations to help them cope with living in the desert, that gives me some time to save something else," Phoebe said.

Everyone else was too tired to even *think* about it.

"But this time it really is an animal in need," Phoebe insisted. "We'll call ourselves S.A.S.H.!"

Phoebe pointed out the window. "S.A.S.H. stands for *Students Against Sleepy Heads*," she said with a giggle.

"Carlos!" we cried. He was still inside the school bus—sound asleep!

"He obviously has no adaptations to cope with desert field trips," Phoebe joked.

Ms. Frizzle smiled. "As I always say, if you can't take the heat, get out of the desert!"

PHOEBE: Hello?

KID: Is this the Magic School Bus?

PHOEBE: Yes, but . . .

KID: Good, because, you see I'm starting a new group . . . S.O.K.R. — *Save Our Kangaroo Rats.* And I want Phoebe to be president.

PHOEBE: You do? I mean, that's nice of you to say, but kangaroo rats don't need to be saved.

KID: You mean they have adaptations that make it possible for them to live in the desert, too.

PHOEBE: Right. For instance, they may never take a drink in their entire lives. They can get all the water they need from the seeds and plants they eat.

KID: One more question! Do you actually know Phoebe?

PHOEBE: Yes, in fact . . .

KID: Could you do me a favor? Just tell her that I think she's the greatest. Good-bye.

Sigh! Maybe I should answer the phone more often.

**All plants, including desert plants, use water.
You can see how by doing this experiment.**

You'll need:

- A white daisy or white carnation
- food coloring
- a glass of water

Put several drops of food coloring into the water until you have a nice, deep color. Then put your flower in the water. In a few days, your flower will change color. It will have absorbed the water through the stem.